A WOMAN'S
BOOK OF FAITH

2,000 Years of Inspirational Writing

By and For Women

EDITED BY M. SHAWN McGARRY

with pencil drawings by
SHARON LUBKEMANN ALLEN

A BIRCH LANE PRESS BOOK
Published by Carol Publishing Group

A Birch Lane Press Book
Published by Carol Publishing Group
is a registered trademark of Carol Communications, Inc.

Editorial, sales and distribution, rights and permissions inquiries should be addressed to Carol Publishing Group, 120 Enterprise Avenue, Secaucus, N.J. 07094

In Canada: Canadian Manda Group, One Atlantic Avenue, Suite 105, Toronto, Ontario M6K 3E7

Carol Publishing books may be purchased in bulk at special discounts for sales promotion, fundraising, or educational purposes. Special editions can be created to specification. For details, contact Special Sales Department, 120 Enterprise Avenue, Secaucus, N.J. 07094.

Original Illustrations by Sharon Lubkemann Allen

Manufactured in the Unied States of America
10 9 8 7 6 5 4 3 2 1

Library of Congress Cataloging-in-Publication Data
A woman's book of faith : 2,000 years of inspirational writing by and for women / edited by M. Shawn McGarry ; with original drawings by Sharon Lubkemann Allen.
        p.   cm.
        "A Birch Lane Press book."
        Includes bibliographical references and index.
ISBN 1–55972–435–8 (hardcover)
1. Women — Religious life. 2. Spiritual life — Quotations, maxims, etc.
3. Women — Quotations. I. McGarry, M. Shawn.
    BL625.7.W6 1997
    242.643 — dc21   97–26535
                                                          CIP

To the girls of El Campo,

*a very present source of hope
and inspiration*

I have learned to live simply, wisely,
To watch the sky and pray to God,
And to roam a while before evening,
To exhaust my needless unease.

Anna Akhmatova, *Rosary* (1912)
Translated by Sharon Lubkemann Allen

CONTENTS

A NOTE TO THE READER

A Woman's Book of Faith is a simple work, founded upon the long, rich tradition of religious writing by women. During the last two thousand years, roughly since the birth of Christianity, women have made significant contributions to the literature of faith. In almost every age and in numerous languages, they have spoken and written about their spiritual experience as women. Though not widely heard, theirs has been a great and ongoing conversation.

The genesis of *A Woman's Book of Faith* goes back to my years as a designer of religious books. I noticed then that a surprising phenomena existed in the religious section of the bookstore. Though women purchased the majority of books on spirituality and religion, they were significantly underrepresented as the writers of such books.

Today, as I look at the *Publishers Weekly* religion list, the situation remains largely the same: men write the majority of religion and spirituality books bought by women. While applauding the written efforts of contemporary men and women, I remain convinced that there is a bevy of wisdom in the older, classic texts by women. In fact, I would suggest that much of the finest spiritual literature written by women was published before this century. Further, these older writings rightly deserve the designation "literature," a term that is not always applicable to modern fare. To supplement this current trend I decided to gather in one volume some of the best spiritual writing by women.

A Woman's Book of Faith is a partial transcript of what history's great-souled women have said and written about their personal faith and its relation to their private and public lives. For practical and historical reasons the readings in this volume come exclusively from the Judeo-Christian tradition.

Placing women from these two traditions side by side in a single volume makes sense for several reasons. First, history connects these two faiths. The New Testament places the origin of Christianity squarely in the Jewish synagogue, in the very bosom of Jewish culture and experience. Such a nexus explains the large body of shared belief in Christianity and Judaism. Second, Jews and Christians share a common religious language grounded in the Old Testament, or Torah. A striking example of this is the recapitulation of poetic language from the *Psalms* and *Proverbs* in the writings of both Jewish and Christian women. In numerous passages writers from both traditions speak of "cleansing the heart," and "restoring the soul." Both plead for God to "order their steps," and be a "light unto their path." Third, both Christian and Jewish women look to the matriarchs of faith such as Eve, Sarah, Rachel and Hagar, Ruth and Naomi, Hannah et cetera, as wise sages and heroines.

Lastly, women from both traditions have faced the same life dilemmas: the death of a child — before or after birth; marriage, childbirth, family life; poverty; the death of a spouse; et cetera. Out of that common experience these women expressed their faith.

These readings require no introduction, literary or theological. In nearly every instance the titles, which were pulled verbatim from the text, adequately announce the selection. To fit the purpose and size of this book it was necessary to keep the readings as concise as possible. Be assured, reader, the gems in this book were mined from a much larger source.

To incarnate the readings, I've written a short biographical sketch of each woman. I have also invited artist and scholar

Sharon Lubkemann Allen to draw a series of ten original por-traits — based almost entirely on historic originals — depict-ing the women of this book. Sharon's drawings capture, almost photographically, the humanity *and* soul life of these women. Many of the originals used by the artist were discov-ered in the Texas Women's University's Edith Dean Collection. Writing in the late fifties, Dean had collected numerous museum prints, intending to publish them in her biography of women. Unfortunately, the publisher could not afford the cost of printing the art with the text of her book.

The portrait of Ruth and Naomi gleaning in the field was based on the artist's imagination and is inspired by a fresh translation of the nineteenth-century Orthodox poet Elizaveta Kuzmina-Karavaeva's *Ruth*.

Finally, since I intended this book to be a kind of informal breviary, I've called the topical index *A Guide to the Readings*. There you will find a thematic map of the readings.

A Woman's Book of Faith is a spiritual compass for women everywhere. I desire that women of all persuasions, alone and in smaller groups, read and re-read the words of this book.

M. Shawn McGarry
Dallas, Texas

PART ONE

The Secret Garden of the Soul

THE SECRET GARDEN OF THE SOUL

Emily Herman

E v e r y soul that is truly alive has a garden of which no other holds the key; and in hours of weariness, when it is breathless with the hot race of life, and harassed by a babel of voices, it slips through the gate and walks at peace among the flowers.

※

Emily Herman (1876–1923), writer, journalist, and wife of a Presbyterian minister, was chiefly concerned with the religious experience of the soul. This selection is taken from her book *The Secret Garden of the Soul and Other Devotional Studies.*

TO BE A GREAT SOUL

Lella Secor

. . . F o r after all, that is what I am striving for more than any-thing else in the world — to be a great soul; to experience life so fully that I shall be able to understand the joys, the aspira-tions, the defeat, the struggle, the discouragements of those around me. For I have come to know that in just such degree as one lives, and experiences, in just that degree one can be of the greatest service to mankind.

※

Lella Secor (1887–1966), raised in the Baptist tradition, was a jour-nalist and peace activist during World War I. She expressed her desire to be a "great soul" in this letter to her mother, dated March 26, 1916.

THE SOUL'S PASSION

Evelyn Underhill

N o w, as the artist's passion for sensuous beauty finds expression in his work, and urges him to create beauty as well as he can, so too the soul's passion for spiritual beauty should find expression in its work; that is to say, in its prayer. . . . [P]rayer ought to be as beautiful as [we] can make it; for thus it approaches more nearly to the mind of God. It should have dignity as well as intimacy, form as well as colour. More, all those little magic thoughts, those delicate winged fancies, which seem like birds rejoicing in God's sight — these, too, should have their place in it.

We find many specimens of them, as it were stuffed and preserved under glass shades, in books of devotion. It is true that their charm and radiance cannot survive this process; the colour now seems crude, the sheen of the plumage is gone. But once these were the living, personal, spontaneous expressions of the love and faith — the inborn poetry — of those from whom they came. Many a liturgic prayer, which now seems to us impersonal and official — foreign to us, perhaps, in its language and thought — will show us, if we have but a little imaginative sympathy, the ardent mood, the exquisite tact, the unforced dignity, of the mind which first composed it; and form a standard by which we may measure our own efforts in this kind.

✸

Evelyn Underhill (1875–1941), writer, lecturer, and wife, was the first woman to be designated an outside lecturer at Oxford University.

IF YOU DON'T BELIEVE IN GOD . . .

Mother Teresa

G O D is everywhere and in everything and without Him we cannot exist. I have never for one moment doubted the existence of God but I know some people do. If you don't believe in God you can help others by doing works of love, and the fruit of these works are the extra graces that come into your soul. Then you'll begin to slowly open up and want the joy of loving God.

※

Mother Teresa (1910–1997), winner of the Nobel Peace Prize, founded the Missionaries of Charity in 1950. Her primary contribution was in work with the world's poorest people.

ALLOW ME TO SPEAK IN YOUR SOUL

Margery Kempe

F O R, daughter, you are as sure of the love of God, as God is God. Your soul is more sure of the love of God than of your own body, for your soul will part from your body, but God shall never part from your soul, for they are united together without end. Therefore, daughter, you have as great a reason to be merry as any lady in this world; and if you knew, daughter, how much you please me when you willingly allow me to speak in you, you would never do otherwise, for this is a holy life and the time is very well spent. For, daughter, this life pleases me more than wearing a coat of mail for penance, or the hair-shirt, or fasting on bread and water; for if you said a thousand *paternosters* every day you would not please me as much as you do when you are in silence and allow me to speak in your soul.

⁂

Margery Kempe (1371–1440) wrote *The Book of Margery Kempe*, the earliest known autobiography of an Englishwoman. The book, lost until 1934, is also one of the most articulate accounts of a Christian life.

ROOTED IN A WOMAN'S HEART

Ray Frank

It may be true that sin came into the world because of the disobedience of the first woman, but woman has long since atoned for it by her loving faith, her blind trust in the Unknown. Down through the ages, traditional and historical, she has come to us the symbol of faith and freedom, of loyalty and love.

From the beginning, she sought knowledge; perceive, it does not say wisdom, but knowledge; and this was at the expense of an Eden. She lost Eden, but she gained the wisdom which has made sure of man's immortality.

She walked upon thorns, she bled; but so sincerely repentant was she, so firmly rooted had become her faith in the Almighty, that no amount of suffering, no change of time and circumstance, could destroy it. With repentance something had sprung up, and blossomed in her being, an imperishable flower, beautiful, fragrant, making the world bright and sweet.

This flower twined itself round man, its odors refreshed and strengthened him; its essence healed him when wounded, and nerved him on to gallant and noble deeds. It is the breath of life in him, and he must needs be careful of its clinging stems, its tender leaves, for they are rooted in a woman's heart.

※

Ray Frank (1865–1948) declined an invitation to be a paid spiritual leader so that she could continue to preach her message of the redemptive nature of home life without the influence of financial motives. Her book *Women in the Synagogue* was published in 1893.

WE ARE RIVERS RUNNING TO THY SEA

Christina Rossetti

LORD, we are rivers running to thy sea,
Our waves and ripples all derived from thee:
A nothing we should have, a nothing be,
    Except for thee.
Sweet are the waters of thy shoreless sea,
Make sweet our waters that make haste to thee;
Pour in thy sweetness, that ourselves may be
    Sweetness to thee.

Christina Rossetti (1830–1894) was an Anglican poet of Italian descent whose sacred verse became internationally popular.

PRAYER AND POETRY

Evelyn Underhill

[T] H E beauty which we seek to incorporate into our spiritual intercourse should not be the dead ceremonious beauty which comes of mere dependence on tradition. It should be the freely upspringing lyric beauty which is rooted in intense personal feeling; the living beauty of a living thing. Nor need we fear the reproach that here we confused religion with poetry. Poetry ever goes like the royal banners before ascending life; therefore man may safely follow its leadership in his prayer, which is — or should be — life in its intensest form. Consider the lilies: those perfect examples of a measured, harmonious, natural and creative life, under a form of utmost loveliness. I cannot help thinking that it is the duty of all Christians to impart something of that flower-like beauty to their prayer. . . .

The springs of the truest prayer and of the most deepest poetry — twin expressions of man's outwardgoing passion for that Eternity which is his home — rise very near together in the heart.

NO FIT TEMPLE

Anne Bradstreet

THAT house which is not often swept makes the cleanly inhabitant soon loathe it; and that heart which is not continually purifying itself is no fit temple for the spirit of God.

Anne Bradstreet (*c.* 1612–1672) was the English-born author of *Contemplations*, a collection of religious poems written for her family. She is considered the first serious poet to write from American soil.

AN UPLIFTING OF THE HEART

Thérèse of Lisieux

F O R me, prayer is an uplifting of the heart, a glance toward Heaven, a cry of gratitude and of love in times of sorrow as well as of joy. It is something noble, something supernatural, which expands the soul and unites it to God.

※

Thérèse of Lisieux (1873–1897), one of the most beloved saints of the modern era, died of tuberculosis at the age of twenty-four. Her autobiography, *The Story of a Soul*, is considered among the Catholic Church's spiritual classics.

Thérèse of Lisieux

MY SOUL LONGS FOR THEE

Julian of Norwich

O GOD, my whole soul longs for Thee. For this is the kind yearnings of the soul by the touching of the Holy Ghost. God, of Thy goodness, give me Thyself; for Thou art enough to me, and I may nothing ask that is less, that may be full worship of Thee; and if I ask anything that is less, ever me wanteth — but only in Thee I have all.

Lord, Thou knowest what I would have. If it be Thy will that I have it, grant it me; and if it be not Thy will, good Lord, be not displeased, for I will not but as Thou willest.

Julian of Norwich (1342–1413), a contemporary of Chaucer, was the first English woman to compose a book on the spiritual life. Dame Julian led a cloistered existence of prayer, contemplation, and devotion to God. Her works were largely unknown before 1902, when *Revelations of Divine Love* was published for the first time.

MY JOYS ARE MYRIAD

Mechthilde of Magdeburg

INTO my soul Thy glory pours like sunlight, edged with gold. Lord, when may my soul at last find rest in Thee? My joys are myriad. My soul is wrapped in Thee and Thou art within my soul as in a garment, yet there must come a time of parting and my heart is filled with pain in the thought of it. If Thou lovedest me more, surely I could depart from here and be where for all eternity I could love Thee as I would! I sing to Thee, yet my song is not as I will it to be. If Thou wouldst sing to me, all imperfection would vanish!

⁂

Mechthilde of Magdeburg (1210–1280) belonged to the Béguines, a community of women who, though dedicated to the religious life, stopped short of taking monastic vows or entering a convent. Her book, *The Flowing Light of God*, is a collection of parables, reflections, and letters written in both prose and verse.

THE SOUL SHINING THROUGH

Jane Porter

BEAUTY of form affects the mind, but then it must not be the mere shell that we admire, but the thought that this shell is only the beautiful case adjusted to the shape and value of a still more beautiful pearl within.

The perfection of outward loveliness is the soul shining through its crystalline covering.

Jane Porter (1776–1850), a Scottish novelist and friend of Sir Walter Scott, published *The Scottish Chiefs* in 1810.

STRIVE TO SEEK SOLITUDE

Teresa of Avila

WE should strive to seek solitude during prayer, in so far as we are able. And God grant that this may suffice to make us realize both the presence of Him who is with us and the answer that our Lord makes to our petitions. Do you think that He is silent, even though we cannot hear Him? Assuredly not! He speaks to the heart when the heart entreats Him.

※

Teresa of Avila (1515–1582), considered one of the greatest religious writers, was the first woman to be given the title Doctor of the Church.

A SIGN IN CALCUTTA

Anonymous

TAKE time to think
Take time to pray
Take time to laugh

It is the source of power
It is the greatest power on earth
It is the music of the soul

Take time to play
Take time to love and be loved
Take time to give

It is the secret of perpetual youth
It is God's given privilege
It is too short a day to be selfish

Take time to read
Take time to be friendly
Take time to work

It is the fountain of wisdom
It is the road to happiness
It is the price of success

Take time to do charity
It is the key to heaven.

PRAYER . . . THE LITTLE IMPLEMENT

Emily Dickinson

P R A Y E R is the little implement
Through which men reach
where Presence is denied them.
They fling their speech
By means of it in God's Ear
If then He hear.
This sums the apparatus
Comprised in prayer.

※

Emily Dickinson (1830–1886), a minister's daughter, is considered one of America's finest poets. Her work was never published in her lifetime.

I HAVE LEARNED TO LIVE SIMPLY

Anna Akhmatova

Translated by Sharon Lubkemann Allen

I HAVE learned to live simply, wisely,
To watch the sky and pray to God,
And to roam a while before evening,
To exhaust my needless unease.

When the burdocks rustle in the ravine
And the yellow-red clusters of mountain ash droop,
I set down merry verses
On ephemeral life, ephemeral and beautiful.

I return. The downy cat
Licks my palm, purrs affectionately,
And the blazing fire kindles
On the turret of the lakeside sawmill.

Only occasionally does the cry of a stork
Landing on the roof slice through the silence.
And were you to knock on my door,
It seems to me, I would not even notice.

※

Anna Akhmatova (1869–1966) was the pseudonym of Anna
Andreyevna Gorenko, the Russian Orthodox writer considered to
be the greatest woman poet in Russian literature.

Anna Akhmatova

FEEL THE NEED FOR PRAYER OFTEN

Mother Teresa

T R Y to feel the need for prayer often during the day and take the trouble to pray. Prayer makes the heart large enough until it can contain God's gift of Himself. Ask and seek, and your heart will grow big enough to receive Him and keep Him as your own.

PART TWO

Prayer . . . the Language of the Soul

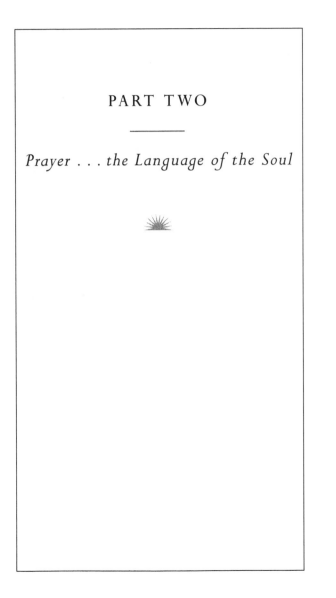

PRAYER IS THE MOST IMPORTANT THING

Sister Kateri

T H E most important thing that a human being can do is pray, because we've been made for God and our hearts are restless until we rest with Him. And it's in prayer that we come into contact with God. We are made for Heaven and we're not going to get to Heaven if we don't pray in *some* way. It doesn't necessarily have to be formal prayer.

※

Sister Kateri is a Missionary of Charity living in New York City.

A MORNING PRAYER

Fanny Neuda

ALL-GRACIOUS, All-merciful God! Thy paternal goodness has permitted me to awaken after a refreshing sleep, and has sent the gladdening rays of morning to revive me anew.

O Heavenly Father! How great is the mercy which Thou hast shown unto me. My first emotion is, therefore, to thank Thee, from the innermost depth of my heart, for Thy providential watchfulness over my life, and for having protected me whilst the darkness of night surrounded me.

How many of my fellow-creatures but yesternight ascended the couch in good health and hopes, and yet cannot leave it this day, from being bound to it by pains and suffering! How many may have yesternight sunk to sleep amidst riches and affluence, but who are brought to poverty this morning by sudden disaster. Alas!

How thankful ought I therefore to be, Heavenly Creator! for Thy goodness, wherewith Thou hast warded off every danger from me, hast preserved my health, and restored me to the arms of my relations and friends. Oh! Let me ever cherish this feeling of gratitude within my heart, so that I may faithfully discharge my religious and domestic duties; that I may meet my fellow-creatures with loving-kindness, such as Thou hast shown unto me; and that I may ever extol Thee, who causest the sleeper to awake, and who wilt cause those that sleep the sleep of death to awake to eternal life. Amen.

✸

Fanny Neuda (nineteenth century) wrote *Hours of Devotion*, a collection of prayers and meditations for use by Jewish women.

ON PRAYER

Madame Jeanne Guyon

I HAVE never found any who prayed so well as those who had never been taught how. They, who have no master in man, have one in the Holy Spirit.

*

Madame Jeanne Guyon (1648–1717), mother of five children and author of more than forty books, was imprisoned for her religious beliefs.

EVERYWHERE I AM IN THY PRESENCE

Susanna Wesley

H E L P me, Lord, to remember that religion is not to be confined to the church or closet, nor exercised only in prayer and meditation, but that everywhere I am in Thy presence. So may my every word and action have a moral content.

As defects and infirmities betray themselves in the daily accidents and common conversations of life, grant me Thy grace, O Lord, that I may watch over, regulate and govern them. Enable me so to know myself and those with whom I have to do, that I may conform to the precepts of the Gospel and train myself to those rules of wisdom and virtue of which I am capable. Help me to discern the proper season and the just occasion of every virtue, and then to apply myself to attain it, by exercising it in those beneficent activities which, for want of due reflection, may not seem of any great importance. May all the happenings of my life prove useful and beneficial to me. May all things instruct me and afford me an opportunity of exercising some virtue and daily learning and growing toward Thy likeness, let the world go which way it will.

⁕

Susanna Wesley (1669–1742), the youngest of twenty-five children, is often credited with being the "mother of Methodism." John Wesley, her fifteenth child, claimed that he learned more from her than "all the theologians in Europe."

HOPE FOR THE HOPELESS

Bridget of Sweden

O MOST sweet Lord Jesus Christ, eternal delight of those who love Thee; joy above all joys we can wish for or desire; firm hope of the hopeless, comforter of the sorrowful and most merciful lover of all penitent sinners, who has said, "My delight is to be with the sons of men," for the love of whom Thou didst in the fullness of time assume human nature; remember, most sweet Lord Jesus, all those sharp sorrows which transpierced Thy sacred soul, from the first instant of Thy incarnation until the time of Thy solitary passion, preordained from all eternity.

☀

Bridget of Sweden (1303–1373), one of Scandinavia's most beloved women, founded the Brigittines, a community of women and men dedicated to a life of simplicity and solitude.

O JOY OF LIFE

Hildegarde of Bingen

O FIRE of God, the Comforter, O life of all that live,
Holy art thou to quicken us, and holy, strength to give:
To heal the broken-hearted ones, their sorest wounds
   to bind,
O Spirit of all holiness, O Lover of mankind! . . .

O surest way, that through the height and through the
   lowest deep
And through the earth dost pass, and all in firmest union
   keep;
From thee the clouds and ether move, from thee the
   moisture flows,
From thee the waters draw their rills, and earth with
   verdure glows.

And thou dost ever teach the wise, and freely on them
   pour,
The inspiration of thy gifts, the gladness of thy lore,
All praise to thee, O joy of life, O hope and strength
   we raise,
Who givest us the prize of light, who art thyself all
   praise.

※

Hildegarde of Bingen (1098–1179) wrote words and music for
more than sixty hymns. Her greatest work, *Know the Ways of the Lord*,
was written over a nine-year period.

A PRAYER OF THANKSGIVING

Queen Elizabeth I

W H E N I survey the evils of this world, in which we thy servants live, and behold the doings of the wicked, the hate of enemies, the dangers and crafty machinations of the impious, and by which we are continually endangered, yet even more when I remember my own life, how many errors and faults have beset me from my youth, I am afraid, I am ashamed and full of despondency. But as soon as I reflect again on thy mighty hand, the greatness and the continuity of thy assistance to me, I resume again my power of reasoning and become more elevated in my hopes. For this reason, coming to thee now with humble heart, I thank thee . . . for all the blessings which thou hast granted to me, thou who, having preserved me from such great dangers and exalted me to the royal throne of this kingdom, hast not ceased to guard me upon it.

. . . Wherefore, confiding in thy unspeakable goodness, I approach and pray thee. . . . my master, my deliverer, King of the universe: sanctify me in soul and in body, in mind and in heart, and renew me wholly. And be to me a helper and protector, ruling in peace my life and my people, thou who alone art blessed everywhere now and for endless ages. Amen.

※

Queen Elizabeth I (1596–1662) composed prayers in Latin and Greek, as well as in English.

GIVE US GRACE

Christina Rossetti

O LORD, give us grace, we beseech Thee, to hear and obey
Thy voice which saith to every one of us, This is the way, walk
ye in it. Nevertheless, let us not hear it behind us saying, This
is the way; but rather before us saying, Follow me. When Thou
puttest us forth, go before us; when the way is too great for
us, carry us; in the darkness of death, comfort us; in the day
of resurrection satisfy us.

※

WALK IN THE WAY OF LOVE

Gertrude More

O MY GOD, let me walk in the way of love which knoweth not how to seek self in anything whatsoever. Let this love wholly possess my soul and heart which, I beseech Thee, may live and move only in, and out of, a pure sincere love for Thee. Oh! That Thy pure love were so grounded and established in my heart that I might sigh and pain without ceasing after Thee, and be able in strength of this Thy love to live without all comfort and consolation, human or divine.

O Lord, give this love into my soul, that I may never more live nor breathe but out of a most pure love of Thee, my All and my only Good. Let me love Thee for Thyself, and nothing else but in and for Thee. Let me love nothing instead of Thee, for to give all for love is a most sweet bargain.

Let Thy love work in and by me, and let me love Thee as Thou wouldst be loved by me. I cannot tell how much love I would have of Thee, because I would love Thee beyond all that can be imagined or desired by me.

Be Thou in this, as in all other things, my chooser for me, for Thou art my only choice most dear to me. The more I shall love Thee, the more will my soul desire Thee, and desire to suffer for Thee.

* * *

Gertrude More (1607–1633) of England followed the Benedictine rule until her death at age twenty-nine. Because of her writings she is considered one of the most important Christian mystics of her time.

ILLUMINATE ME

Vittoria Colonna

G R A N T, I pray, O Lord, that with that lowliness of mind that befits my humble condition, and that elevation of soul which Your majesty demands, I may ever adore You; may I continually live in that fear which Your justice inspires, in that hope which Your clemency permits. May I submit myself to You as all-powerful, leave myself in Your hand, as all-wise, and turn unto You as all-perfect and good. I beseech You, most merciful Father, that Your most vivid fire may purify me, that Your clearest light may illuminate me, and that purest love of Yours may so advance me that, held back by no mortal influence, I may return safe and happy to You.

※

Vittoria Colonna (1490–1547) inspired Italian artist Michelangelo with her dedication to the simplicity of the Christian faith.

DRAW ME TO THYSELF

Gertrude of Helfta

D R A W me and unite me entirely to Thyself, that I may remain inseparably attached to Thee, even when I am obliged to attend to exterior duties for the good of my neighbor and that afterwards I may return again to seek Thee within me, when I have accomplished them for Thy glory, in the most perfect manner possible, even as the winds, when agitated by a tempest, return again to their former calm when the tempest has ceased; that Thou mayest find me as zealous in laboring for Thee as Thou hast been assiduous in helping me; and that, by this means, mayest Thou elevate me to the highest degree of perfection to which Thy justice can permit Thy mercy to raise so carnal and rebellious a creature.

☀

Gertrude of Helfta (1256–1302), a theologian and mystic also known as Gertrude the Great, wrote *The Herald of Divine Love*.

GOD'S ANSWERS

Elizabeth Barrett Browning

G O D answers sharp and sudden on some prayers,
And thrusts the thing we have prayed for in our face,
A gauntlet with a gift in't.

✺

Elizabeth Barrett Browning (1806–1861) wrote *Sonnets From the Portuguese*, a collection of romantic poetry. She married the poet Robert Browning in 1846.

Elizabeth Barrett Browning

FAITH AND WORKS TOGETHER GROW

Hannah More

I F faith produce no works, I see
  That faith is not a living tree:
Thus faith and works together grow;
  No separate life they e'er can know;
They're soul and body, hand and heart —
  What God hath joined, let no man part.

※

Hannah More (1745–1833), an English educator and writer, composed religious pamphlets for the poor. In one year, two million such "tracts" — sold for a penny each — were distributed.

BE THOU MY GUIDE

Fraunces Aburgauenny

F R O M sinfulness preserve me, Lord,
R enew my spirit in my hart;
A nd let my tongue therwith accord,
U ttering all goodness for his part.
N o thought let there arise in me
C ontrarie to thy precepts ten;
E ver let me most mindful be
S till for to praise they name, Amen.
A s of my soul, so of my bodie,
B e thou my guider, O my God!
U nto thee only do I crie,
R emove from mee thy furious rod.
G raunt that my head may still devise
A ll things that pleasing be to thee.
U nto mine ears, and to mine eies,
E ver let there a watch set bee,
N one ill that they may heare and see;
N o wicked deed let my hand do,
Y n thy good paths let my feet go.

*

Fraunces Aburgauenny (sixteenth century), also known as Lady
Bergauenny, wrote prose and poetry. The acrostic poem above was
her contribution to *The Monument of Matrons*, published in 1582.

THE LANGUAGE OF THE HEART

Grace Aguilar

Hear O Israel! The Lord Our God . . . The Lord is One.

THERE is one portion of the Jewish form of prayer, which every member of that nation is desired to repeat twice, sometimes three times, in every day. It is first taught to our children; either in Hebrew or in English, the words of the *Shemang* [Sh'ma] are the first ideas of prayers which the infant mind receives, long before any meaning can be attached to them; and it is right that it should be so; for so much of vital importance is contained in this brief portion of our ritual, that we cannot impress it too early on the heart of an Israelite. . . . It contains no actual prayer, but prayer is a word which may be taken in a wider sense than its literal meaning. For prayer is the language of the heart, — needing no measured voice, no spoken tone; thus Hannah's wish was heard and answered, though not a sound passed her lips. It is the hour of communion between man and Maker — the hour granted to the fallen man to lift him above this world, to bring his great Creator, his merciful Father, a while from His lofty throne above the heavens, even to his side, listening in mercy to his anguished cry, healing the open wound, bidding the floods of woe subside, and leaving His blessed Spirit on the soul to encourage and soothe.

※

Grace Aguilar (1816–1847) wrote *The Spirit of Judaism* in 1842. She wished it to be read by both Christian and Jewish women as her message was one of commonality and shared belief.

I HEAR THE VOICE OF GOD

Anna Laetitia Barbauld

I READ God's awful name emblazon'd high,
With golden letters on th' illumin'd sky;
Nor less the mystic characters I see,
Wrought in each flower, inscribed on ev'ry tree;
In ev'ry leaf that trembles on the breeze
I hear the voice of God among the trees.
With thee in shady solitudes I walk,
With thee in busy crowded cities talk;
In every creature own thy forming power,
In each event thy providence adore.

Thy hopes shall animate my drooping soul,
Thy precepts guide me, and thy fear control:
From anxious cares, from gloomy terrors free,
And feel myself omnipotent in thee.

That when the last, the closing hour draws nigh,
And earth recedes before my swimming eye;
Teach me to quit this transitory scene
With decent triumph and a look serene;
Teach me to fix my ardent hopes on high,
And, having lived to thee, in thee to die.

❋

Anna Laetitia Barbauld (1743–1825), author of *Hymns in Prose for Children*, was an English writer, editor, and poet who is remembered for her meditative verse.

FOR WHAT SHALL I PRAISE THEE?

Elizabeth Fry

F O R what shall I praise thee, my God and my King,
For what blessings the tribute of gratitude bring?
Shall I praise thee for pleasure, for health, and for ease,
For the spring of delight, and the sunshine of peace?

Shall I praise thee for flowers that bloomed on my breast,
For joys in perspective, and pleasures possessed,
For the spirits that brightened my days of delight,
For the slumbers that sat on my pillow at night?

For this I would praise thee; but if only for this,
I should leave half untold the donation of bliss:
I thank thee for sickness, for sorrow, for care,
For the thorns I have gathered, the anguish I bear.

For nights of anxiety, watching, and tears —
A present of pain, a perspective of fears;
I praise thee, I bless thee, my King and my God,
For the good and the evil thy hand hath bestowed.

The flowers were sweet, but their fragrance is flown;
They yielded no fruits, they are withered and gone:
The thorn it was poignant, but precious to me,
'Twas the message of mercy — it led me to thee!

Elizabeth Fry (1780–1845), a Quaker philanthropist, used space in
her home to educate poor children. Later in life she spent much of
her time organizing prison visitations and bringing a message of
hope to the incarcerated.

DISPOSE OUR HEARTS

Jane Austen

FATHER of Heaven! Whose goodness has brought us in safety to the close of this day, dispose our hearts in fervent prayer. Another day is now gone, and added to those, for which we were before accountable. Teach us, Almighty Father, to consider this solemn truth, as we should do, that we may feel the importance of every day, and every hour as it passes, and earnestly strive to make a better use of what Thy goodness may yet bestow on us, than we have done of the time past.

Jane Austen (1775–1817) was a rector's daughter whose novels of family life gave the English novel its distinctly modern form. Her *Evening Prayers*, bearing a date of 1818, were not published in her lifetime.

LOVE LEADS TO CONTEMPLATION

Angela of Foligno

O T H O U, supreme Good, who hast deigned to show us that Thou art Love, Thou also makest us to be in love with this Love; wherefore they who come before Thy face shall be rewarded according to the measure of their Love. There is nothing which leadeth the contemplative unto contemplation, save true love alone.

Angela of Foligno (1248–1309) founded a community of Sisters of Charity. Her brilliant writing earned her the sobriquet "Teacher of Theologians."

CIRCUMSTANCES GREAT AND SMALL

Queen Anne

A L M I G H T Y and Eternal God, the Disposer of all the affairs of the world, there is not one circumstance so great as not to be subject to Thy power, nor so small but it comes within Thy care; Thy goodness and wisdom show themselves through all Thy words, and Thy loving-kindness and mercy appear in the several dispensations of Thy Providence. May we readily submit ourselves to Thy pleasure and sincerely resign our wills to Thine, with all patience, meekness and humility.

Queen Anne of Great Britain and Ireland (1665–1714), a Protestant by tradition, is remembered for her devoted labors in and for the Church of England.

THE MORE I FIND THE MORE I SEEK

Catherine of Siena

Y o u, O eternal trinity, are a deep sea into which, the more I enter, the more I find, and the more I find, the more I seek. O abyss, O eternal Godhead, O sea profound, what more could you give me than yourself?

Catherine of Siena (1347–1380), the twenty-third child of an Italian cloth dyer, served the sick and dying during the Black Death. Her written works include *Book of Divine Doctrine*, which is often compared to Dante's *Divine Comedy* in its expression of the soul's union with God.

Catherine of Siena

THE LOVELY ORNAMENT OF HUMILITY

Anne Steele

GRACIOUS God, who wilt, with the most inestimable gift of Thy love, freely give us all things which we need, O give me more and more the lovely ornament of humility! Enable me to meditate with delightful attention on the excellencies of my Saviour and ardently desire to be more like him in this engaging virtue! O how bright it shone in every scene of His astonishing abasement! And did the holy Jesus, the Lord of Lords and King of Kings, condescend to innumerable instances of benevolence to poor sinners! Did he even stoop to wash the feet of His disciples, to teach them a lesson of affectionate humility! And shall not I, a poor sinful creature, rejoice to be able to administer any comfort or assistance to the meanest of His servants? Transform me, blessed Saviour, into Thy own lovely image, and make me meek and lowly.

※

Anne Steele (1717–1778), a beloved English writer of Baptist hymns, lost her fiancé to drowning a few hours before their wedding ceremony.

ADORE THE MYSTERY

Susanna Wesley

I PRAISE Thee, O God, for illuminating my mind and for enabling me to prove demonstratively that Thy wisdom is as infinite as Thy power. Help me to use these discoveries to praise and love and obey, and may I be exceedingly careful that my affections keep pace with my knowledge.

May I adore the mystery I cannot comprehend. Help me to be not too curious in prying into those secret things that are known only to Thee, O God, not too rash in censuring what I do not understand. May I not perplex myself about those methods of providence that seem to me involved and intricate, but resolve them into Thine infinite wisdom, who knowest the spirit of all flesh and dost best understand how to govern those souls Thou hast created.

We are of yesterday and know nothing. But Thy boundless mind comprehends, at one view, all things, past, present and future, and as Thou dost see all things, Thou dost best understand what is good and proper for each individual and for me, with relation to both worlds. So deal with me, O my God.

※

SANCTIFYING LIFE'S PLEASURES

Madame de Maintenon

O LORD, my God, Thou has placed me where I am. I desire to worship during all my life Thy providential dispensations towards me, and I submit myself to them without reserve. Give me, O my God, the grace fit for the estate to which Thou hast called me, that I may bear in a Christian way its weariness, that I may sanctify its pleasures, that I may seek in all things Thy glory, that I may uphold that glory before the princes among whom Thou hast placed me, and that I may minister to the King's salvation.

Let me never give way to the trouble and restlessness of an unquiet mind, which grows weary and slackens in the duties of its state, envying the fancied happiness of other conditions of life. May Thy will and not mine be done, O Lord!

Thou who holdest the hearts of kings in Thy hand, open the King's heart that I may instil into it the good Thou desirest; and grant that I may please him, comfort him, strengthen him and even afflict him, when it shall be for Thy glory. Grant that I may never hide from him what he ought to know through me, and which others may not have the courage to tell him. Grant that I may be saved with him, that I may love him in Thee and for Thee, and that he may love me in the same way. Grant us to walk together in Thy justice, without reproach till the day of Thy coming.

☀

Madame de Maintenon (1635–1719) founded an educational institution for impoverished girls near Paris, France.

GOD'S INNUMERABLE PERFECTIONS

Teresa of Avila

O ABSOLUTE Sovereign of the world! Thou art Supreme Omnipotence, Sovereign Goodness, Wisdom itself! Thou art without beginning and without end. Thy works are limitless, Thy perfections infinite, and Thy intelligence is supreme! Thou art a fathomless abyss of marvels! O Beauty, containing all other beauty! O great God, Thou art Strength itself! Would that I possessed at this moment all the combined eloquence and wisdom of men! Then, in as far as it is possible here below, where knowledge is so limited, I could strive to make known one of Thy innumerable perfections. The contemplation of these reveals to some extent the nature of Him who is our Lord and our only Good.

MAKE ME TO STAND FIRM

Margaret of Antioch

O Lord God, ruler of heaven and of the earth, creator of things visible and invisible, giver of eternal life, and consoler of the sorrowful, make me to stand firm in the confession of Thy name that as with Thine aid I have begun the good fight, so with Thine aid I may be deemed worthy to gain the victory, lest the adversary spitefully mock at me, saying: "Where is now her God in whom she trusted?"

But let the angel of Thy light come and restore to me the light which the darkness of my cell has taken from me; and let the right hand of Thy majesty scatter the phantom hosts of the ancient enemy. For we know, O Lord, that Thy mercy will aid us in all temptations.

※

Margaret of Antioch (third century) was beheaded under Roman emperor Diocletian. Many consider her the patron saint of expectant mothers.

ALL HONEST WORK IS A PRAYER

Evelyn Underhill

[W] H A T do we mean by prayer? Surely just this: that part of our active and conscious life which is deliberately orientated towards, and exclusively responds to, spiritual reality. The Being of God, Who is that spiritual reality, we believe to be immanent in all things: "He is not far from each one of us: for in Him we live, and move, and have our being." Therefore in attending to those visible and concrete things, we are in a way attending to that immanent God; and in this sense all honest work is indeed, as the old proverb says, a sort of prayer. But when we speak of prayer as a separate act or activity of the self, we mean more than this. We mean, in fact, as a rule the other aspect of spiritual experience and communion; in the language of theology, attention to transcendent rather than to immanent Reality. Prayer, says Walter Hilton "is nothing else but an ascending or getting up of the desire of the heart into God, by withdrawing it from all earthly thoughts."

★

THE POWER OF JOY AND SUFFERING

Simone Weil

J o y and suffering are two equally precious gifts which must both of them be fully tasted, each one in its purity and without trying to mix them. Through joy, the beauty of the world penetrates our soul. Through suffering it penetrates our body. We could no more become friends of God through joy alone than one becomes a ship's captain by studying books on navigation. . . . In order that our being may one day become wholly sensitive in every part to this obedience which is the substance of matter, in order that a new sense may be formed in us which allows us to hear the universe as the vibration of the word of God, the transforming power of suffering and of joy are equally indispensable. When either of them comes to us we have to open the very centre of our soul to it, as a woman opens her door to messengers from her beloved. What does it matter to a lover if the messenger is courteous or rough so long as he gives her a message?

.

※

Simone Weil (1909–1943) was raised in a Jewish home but leaned more toward Christianity in her later years. Much of her voluminous writing addresses the related mysteries of suffering and redemption.

ORDER MY STEPS

Queen Elizabeth I

H o w exceeding is thy goodness, and how great mine offences! Of nothing hast thou made me, not a worm, but a Creature according to thine own image, heaping all the blessings upon me that men on earth hold most happy. . . . And above all this, making me (though a weak woman) yet thy instrument. . . .

Now for these and other thy benefits (O Lord of all goodness) what have I rendered to thee? Forgetfulness, unthankfulness and great disobedience. I should have magnified thee. I have neglected thee. I should have prayed unto thee. I have forgotten thee. I should have served thee. I have sinned against thee. This is my case. Then where is my hope? But thou art gracious and merciful, long suffering and of great goodness, not delighting in the death of a Sinner. Thou seest whereof I came, of corrupt seed, what I am, a most frail substance: where I live, in the world full of wickedness: where delights be snares, where dangers be imminent, where sin reigneth, and death abideth. This is my state.

Now where is my comfort?. . . Create a clean heart, renew a right spirit within me. Order my steps in thy word, that no wickedness have dominion over me, make me obedient to thy will and [to] delight in thy law. Grant me grace to live godly and to govern justly: that so living to please thee, and reigning to serve thee, I may ever glorify thee the Father of all goodness and mercy. . . . Amen.

NO MORE FEAR OF DEATH

Macrina the Younger

O LORD, Thou hast taken from us the fear of death; Thou makest the close of life, the commencement of a new and truer life. For a while Thou wilt suffer our bodies to sleep, and then will call us with the trumpet at the end of time.

Now send Thee an angel of light besides me; bid him take my hand and lead me to the place of rest, where there is water for my thirst beside the dwelling place of the Holy Fathers.

If in the weakness of the flesh I have sinned in word, or deed, or thought, forgive me Thou, O Lord, for Thou hast power to forgive sins on earth. When I am divested of my body, may I stand before Thee with my soul unspotted; receive it, Thou, without faults or sins, in Thine own hands.

*

Macrina the Younger (327–379) founded a religious community for women in the Eastern Church.

FROM THEE ALL BLESSINGS COME

Coretta Scott King

ETERNAL and everlasting God, who art the Father of all mankind, as we turn aside from the hurly-burly of everyday living, may our hearts and souls, yea, our very spirits, be lifted upward to thee, for it is from thee that all blessings come.

Coretta Scott King, wife of the late Martin Luther King Jr., lives in Atlanta, Georgia.

GIVE ME A LIVELY FAITH

Clare of Assisi

GLORY and praise be to Thee,
Most loving Jesus Christ!

From all evils, past,
Present and to come,
Deliver me!

Do Thou, by Thy most bitter death,
Give me a lively faith, firm hope
A perfect charity,

That with my whole soul I may love Thee,
With all my soul,
With all my strength.

Firm and steadfast in good works
Make me, and in Thy service
Make to persevere,

So that I may be able always
To please Thee,
Lord Jesus Christ.

※

Clare of Assisi (1194–1253) cofounded the "Poor Clares," a
women's order founded upon a life of simplicity and detachment
from wealth of any type.

Clare of Assisi

AN ABUNDANCE OF PEACE

Brigid of Ireland

I WOULD like the Angels of Heaven to be amongst us.
I would like the abundance of peace.
I would like full vessels of charity.
I would like rich treasures of mercy.
I would like cheerfulness to preside over all.
I would like the friends of Heaven to be gathered around
us from all parts.
I would like myself to be a rent-payer to the Lord; that I
should suffer distress and that He would bestow a good
blessing upon me.

※

Brigid of Ireland (c. 453–c. 523), one of Ireland's most cherished
women, founded her country's first nunnery at Kildare.

PRAYER OF THANKSGIVING

Catherine of Siena

THANKS, thanks to Thee, O eternal Father, for Thou hast not despised me, the work of Thy hands, nor turned Thy face from me, nor despised my desires!

Thou, the light, hast not regarded my darkness. Thou, true life, hast not regarded my living death. Thou, the physician, hast not been repelled by my grave infirmities. Thou, the eternal purity, hast not considered the many miseries of which I am full. Thou, who art the infinite, hast overlooked that I am finite. Thou, who art wisdom, hast overlooked my folly.

AN EVENING PRAYER

Susanna Wesley

I GIVE Thee praise, O God, for a well-spent day. But I am yet unsatisfied, because I do not enjoy enough of Thee. I would have my soul more closely united to Thee by faith and love. I would love Thee above all things. Thou, who hast made me, knowest my desires, my expectations. My joys all centre in Thee and it is Thou Thyself that I desire; it is Thy favour, Thine acceptance, the communications of Thy grace that I earnest wish for, more than anything in the world. I rejoice in Thine essential glory and blessedness. I rejoice in my relation to Thee, who art my Father, my Lord and my God. I rejoice that Thou hast power over me and that I desire to live in subjection to Thee. I thank Thee that Thou hast brought me so far. I will beware of despairing of Thy mercy for the time which is to come, and will give Thee the glory of Thy free grace. Amen.

Susanna Wesley

GUARD US THIS NIGHT

Jane Austen

B E gracious to our necessities, and guard us, and all we love, from evil this night. May the sick and afflicted, be now, and ever thy care; and heartily do we pray for the safety of all that travel by land or by sea, for the comfort and protection of the orphan and widow and that thy pity may be shewn upon all captives and prisoners.

Above all other blessings Oh! God, for ourselves, and our fellow-creatures, we implore thee to quicken our sense of Thy mercy in the redemption of the world, of the value of that holy religion in which we have been brought up, that we may not, by our own neglect, throw away the salvation thou hast given us. . . . Hear us almighty God, for His sake who has redeemed us, and taught us thus to pray.

PART THREE

Faith, Home, and Family

THE HOME: A CENTER OF COMPASSION

Mother Teresa

W E must make our homes centers of compassion and forgive endlessly.

THE RAPTURE OF MATERNAL LOVE

Grace Aguilar

W E R E love and gratitude to [God] banished from every other human heart, surely they would swell in a young mother's breast, as she gazes upon the little creature undeniably His gift, and feels the full gushing tide of rapture ever attendant on maternal love. Surely in such a moment there must be whisperings of devotion, leading the soul in gratitude to the beneficent Giver of her babe, or swelling it with prayer to guide that precious charge aright. It may be, that doubts of her own capability of executing a task, as solemnly important as inexpressibly sweet, may naturally arise; but these doubts, instead of leading her to give up the task in despair, should lead her to the footstool of her God in prayer; and her petition, even as that of Hannah was, will be granted.

OVER WASH-TUB AND IRONING TABLE

Amanda Smith

O N E day I was busy with my work and thinking and communing with Jesus, for I found out that it was not necessary to be a nun or be isolated away off in some deep retirement to have communion with Jesus; but, though your hands are employed in doing your daily business, it is no bar to the soul's communion with Jesus. Many times over my wash-tub and ironing table, and while making my bed and sweeping my house and washing my dishes I have had some of the richest blessings. Oh, how glad I am to know this, and how many mothers' hearts I have cheered when I told them that the blessing of sanctification did not mean isolation from all the natural and legitimate duties of life, as some seem to think. Not at all. It means God in you, supplying all your needs according to His riches in glory by Christ Jesus; our need of grace and patience and long suffering and forbearance, for we have to learn how not only to bear, but also to forbear with infirmities of ourselves and others as well.

Amanda Smith (1837–1915), born a slave, received international recognition as a pioneer black missionary-evangelist. Her spiritual autobiography, *The Lord's Dealings with Mrs. Amanda Smith*, was among the first written by an African American.

THE SONG OF MARY

Mary, Mother of Jesus

A N D Mary said:

My soul magnifies the Lord,
And my spirit has rejoiced
   In God my Savior.
For He has regarded the lowly state
   Of His maidservant;
For behold, henceforth all generations
   Will call me blessed.
For He who is mighty has done
   Great things for me,
And holy is His name.
And His mercy is on those
   Who fear Him
From generation to generation.
He has shown strength with His arm;
He has scattered the proud in the
   Imagination of their hearts.
He has put down the mighty
   From their thrones,
And exalted the lowly.
He has filled the hungry
   With good things,
And the rich He has sent away empty.

He has helped His servant Israel,
In remembrance of His mercy,
As He spoke to our fathers,
To Abraham and to his seed forever.

***

Mary, Mother of Jesus, Jewish by birth, is perhaps the most cele-brated woman in the Christian tradition. The above selection, the *Magnificat*, exhibits Mary's fondness for the Old Testament in its numerous quotations from and allusion to that sacred text.

MOTHER, WIFE, SISTER, SWEETHEART

Ray Frank

IN MOTHER, wife, sister, sweetheart, lies the most precious part of man. In them he sees perpetual reminders of the death-sin, guarantees of immortality. Think, woman, what your existence means to man; dwell well on your responsibility.

THE HOME AS SYNAGOGUE

Mary M. Cohen

THERE is very little doubt that the idea with which the Jewish religion was planned was to so engraft it upon the home life that the two should be inseparably joined. The observances of the faith are so entwined with the every-day atmosphere of the home as to make the Jewish religion and the family life one, a bond in sanctity. In this sense the synagogue is the home, and the home the synagogue. I mean that the intelligent and devout Hebrew parent is the priest or priestess of the family altar. There is no need, if there is a desire to worship the God of Israel, to visit the sanctuary; it is always right and appropriate to enter the House of God, but it is never indispensable for the performance of religious service. . . .

The greatest benefit derived from this close connection between the religion and life is the fact that the religion thus became an intensely practical one, and yet lost nothing of its inspired ideality.

※

Mary M. Cohen (1854–1911) was a poet and essayist who stressed the interconnectedness of spirituality and family life.

PROTECT MY NEWBORN INFANT

Fanny Neuda

. . . H o w dark was everything around me but a few hours ago; anxiety filled my heart, and I was afraid of the results of my fears and pain. But when I called in my woe, the Lord heard me, and saved me from my troubles. The hours of anxiety have passed, and now joy and light surrounded me. Thou, O God! hast safely led me through the dangers of the hour of delivery, Thou has done more unto me than I ventured to hope; Thou hast fulfilled my prayer, Thou hast given me a dear, healthful, well-formed child. Therefore, I praise Thy mercy, and shall never forget Thy benefits; my heart and mouth shall ever overflow with thanks and praises of Thy supreme power and loving-kindness.

And with filial confidence in Thy mercy I commit all my cares unto Thee, trusting that Thou wilt accomplish the work of grace which Thou has commenced. Thou wilt renew my strength, that I may be able to fulfil the duties of a good and faithful mother.

My God and Lord! Bestow Thy protection also upon my newborn infant, that it may thrive and grow, and be healthful in body and soul, to be a pleasure unto Thee, a delight unto me and my beloved husband, an honor unto all men.

ADVICE TO MY CHILDREN

Glückel of Hameln

ABOVE all, my children, be honest in money matters. . . .
If you have in hand money or goods belonging to other people, give more care to them than if they were your own, so
that, please God, you do no one a wrong. The first question
put to a man in the next world is, whether he was faithful in
his business dealings. Let a man work ever so hard amassing
great wealth dishonestly, let him during his lifetime provide
his children fat dowries and upon his death a rich heritage —
yet woe, I say, and woe again to the wicked who for the sake
of enriching his children has lost his share in the world to
come! For the fleeting moment he has sold Eternity.

※

Glückel of Hameln (1646—1724), a wife, mother, and business-
woman, wrote her memoirs for the instruction and benefit of her
adult children. Hers is the earliest memoir by a Jewish woman.

A PRAYER FOR THE NEW MILLENNIUM

Williamina Forbes Leith

O G o d, we beseech You, mercifully to receive our prayers, and grant that we may both perceive what things we ought to do, and also, may have the grace and power faithfully to fulfill the same, knowing that by You the whole world is governed and preserved. We are Your erring creatures, and under a thankful sense of Your providential care we now draw near to You, to offer up as a family our humble sacrifice of prayer and praise. . . .

Williamina Forbes Leith (nineteenth century) published a collection of prayers written for her children in 1839. In a short time, the prayers became popular in several religious circles, as well as the military, where her husband was a colonel.

MY MOTHER

Amanda Smith

MOTHER was very thoughtful and scrupulously economical. She could get up the best dinner out of almost nothing of anybody I ever saw in my life. She often cheered my father's heart when he came home at night and said: "Well, mother, how have you got on today?"

"Very well," she would say. It was hard planning sometimes; yet we children never had to go to bed hungry. After our evening meal, so often of nice milk and mush, she would call us children and make us all say our prayers before we went to bed. I never remember a time when I went to bed without saying the Lord's Prayer as it was taught me by my mother. Even before we were free I was taught to say my prayers.

TO MY HUSBAND

Eliza

W H E N from the world, I shall be tane,
And from earths necessary paine,
Then let no blacks be worne for me,
Not in a Ring my dear by thee.
But this bright Diamond, let it be
Worn in rememberance of me.
And when it sparkles in your eye,
Think 'tis my shadow passeth by.
For why, more bright you shall me see,
Then that or any Gem can bee.
Dress not the house with sable weed,
As if there were some dismall deed
Acted to be when I am gone,
There is no cause for me to mourn.
And let no badge of Herald be
The signe of my Antiquity.
It was my glory I did spring
From heavens eternall powerfull King:
To his bright Palace heir am I.
It is his promise, hee'l not lye.
By my dear Brother pray lay me,
It was a promise made by thee,
And now I must bid thee adieu,
For I'me a parting now from you.

Although Eliza's identity is unknown, the title page of her 1652
book suggests a devout soul: "Written by a Lady, who only desires
to advance the glory of God, and not her own."

ON PARENTING

Glückel of Hameln

A BIRD was once set out to cross a windy sea with its three fledglings. The sea was so wide and the wind so strong, the father bird was forced to carry his young, one by one, in his strong claws. When he was half-way across with the first fledgling the wind turned to a gale, and he said, "My child, look how I am struggling and risking my life in your behalf. When you are grown up, will you do as much for me and provide for my old age?" The fledgling replied, "Only bring me to safety, and when you are old I shall do everything you ask of me." Whereat the father bird dropped his child into the sea, and it drowned, and he said, "So shall it be done to such a liar as you." Then the father bird returned to shore, set forth with his second fledgling, asked the same question, and receiving the same answer, drowned the second child with the cry, "You, too, are a liar!" Finally he set out with the third fledgling, and when he asked the same question, the third and last fledgling replied, "My dear father, it is true you are struggling mightily and risking your life in my behalf, and I shall be wrong not to repay you when you are old, but I cannot bind myself. This though I can promise: when I am grown up and have children of my own, I shall do as much for them as you have done for me." Whereupon the father bird said, "Well spoken, my child, and wisely; your life I will spare and I will carry you to shore in safety."

A LETTER TO MY SON

Yette Beckman

M y dear Son:

The long-expected has come to pass — your trip to America. You realize, my dear son, the heart pangs I suffer at the thought of your going. It is your wish, and so shall it be. May the Almighty guide and protect you from all evil and always be with you.

Put your trust in Him and He will lead you in the right way. Be brave and good and continue your filial affection. Do not forget our sacred religion. It will bring you comfort and consolation; it will teach you patience and endurance, no matter how trying the circumstances or difficult the trial.

Whether your life be one of success or of struggle, whether rich or poor, keep God before your eyes and in your heart.

You are going out into the wide world, far from parents, brothers, or sisters. It will be trying for you, but you are blessed with many good qualities, and my heart is confident that no harm will befall you. Commit your way unto the Lord and He will bring it to pass.

Be careful in your business associations, and particularly in forming friendships. Above all, guard your health, for that is the greatest gift on earth

I would like to and I could say much more to you, my dear son — but it is very distressing for me. I only say:

"Travel with God, be ever cheerful and courageous, and put to good use all that you have been taught."

Though a great distance separates us, and you are far from parental care, my thought of you will never cease so long as my heart beats. . . .

Your ever faithful,

Mother

＊

Yette Beckman (nineteenth century), a German Jew, dated this letter to her son "11 P.M., 30 September 1880."

PRAYER IN FAMILIES

Mother Teresa

PRAYER is needed for children and in families. Love begins at home and that is why it is important to pray together. If you pray together you will stay together and love each other as God loves each one of you. Whatever religion we are, we must pray together. Children need to learn to pray and they need to have their parents pray with them. If we don't do this, it will be difficult to become holy, to carry on, to strengthen ourselves in faith.

Mother Teresa

THE BEST THING FOR MY CHILDREN

Glückel of Hameln

T H E best thing for you, my children, is to serve God from your heart, without falsehood or sham, not giving out to people that you are one thing while, God forbid, in your heart you are another. Say your prayers with awe and devotion. During the time for prayers, do not stand about and talk of other things. While prayers are being offered to the Creator of the world, hold it a great sin to engage another man in talk about an entirely different matter — shall God Almighty be kept waiting until you have finished your business?

INSTRUCTING YOUNG CHILDREN

Grace Aguilar

To instruct young children in the dull routine of daily lessons, to force the wandering mind to attention, the unwilling spirit to subjection, to bear with natural disinclination to irksome tasks, all this . . . is far more attractive in theory than in practice. It is a drudgery for which even some mothers themselves have not sufficient patience. . . . [But] to speak of God, to teach the child His will, to instil His love into the infant heart, should never be looked on as a daily task, nor associated with all the dreaded paraphernalia of books and lessons. The Bible should be the guide to, and assistance in, this precious employment.

※

MARY AT THE CROSS

Harriet Beecher Stowe

O WONDROUS Mother! since the dawn of time
    Was ever love, was ever grief, like thine?
O highly favored in thy joy's deep flow,
    And favored even in this, thy bitterest woe!
Poor was that home in simple Nazareth
    Where, fairly growing, like some silent flower,
Last of a kingly race, unknown and lowly,
    O desert lily, passed thy childhood's hour.
The world knew not the tender, serious maiden.
    Who through deep loving years so silent grew,
Full of high thought and holy aspiration,
    Which the o'ershadowing God alone might view.
And then it came, that message from the highest,
    Such as to woman ne'er before descended,
The Almighty wings thy prayerful soul o'erspread,
    And with thy life the Life of worlds was blended.
Blest through those thirty years, when in thy dwelling
    He lived a God disguised with unknown power;
And thou his sole adorer, his best love,
    Trusting, revering, waited for his hour.
Now by that corss thou tak'st thy final station,
    And shar'st the last dark trial of thy Son;

Not with weak tears or woman's lamentation,
　　But with high silent anguish like his own.
All now is darkness; and in that deep stillness
　　The God-man wrestles with that might woe;
Hark to that cry, the rock of ages rending, —
　　" 'Tis finished!" Mother, all is glory now!

Harriet Beecher Stowe (1811–1896), the daughter of a Con-
gregationalist minister, is best known for *Uncle Tom's Cabin*, the
antislavery novel that helped to spark the Civil War.

PART FOUR

The Challenges of Faith

SONG ABOUT A SONG

Anna Akhmatova

Translated by Sharon Lubkemann Allen

It burns at first,
Like an icy breath,
And then sinks into the heart
Like a single salty tear.

And a spiteful heart will begin to regret
Something. It will be sad.
But it will not forget
this slight sorrow.

I only sow. Others
Will reap. So be it!
This triumphant host of harvesters
Bless, O God!

And so that I may thank You
I will be utterly bold,
Give me leave to render to the world
That which is more imperishable than love.

SIFTING OUT THE HEARTS

Julia Ward Howe

M I N E eyes have seen the glory of the coming of the
  Lord;
he is trampling out the vintage where the grapes of wrath
  are stored;
he hath loosed the fateful lightning of his terrible swift
  sword;
his truth is marching on.

I have seen him in the watch-fires of a hundred circling
  camps;
they have builded him an altar in the evening dews and
  damps;
I can read his righteous sentence by the dim and flaring
  lamp;
his day is marching on.

He has sounded forth the trumpet that shall never call
  retreat;
he is sifting out the hearts of men before his judgment
  seat;
O be swift, my soul, to answer him! Be jubilant, my feet;
Our God is marching on.

In the beauty of the lilies Christ was born across the sea;
with a glory in his bosom that transfigures you and me;
as he died to make men holy, let us live to make men
     free,
while God is marching on.

☀

Julia Ward Howe (1819—1910) was the social reformer who insti-
tuted what we call Mother's Day. Her *Battle Hymn of the Republic* was
published in the February, 1862 issue of the *Atlantic Monthly*.

THESE LINGERING MINUTES

Elizabeth Rowe

R O L L faster on, ye lingering minutes: the nearer my joys, the more impatient I am to seize them: after these painful agonies, how greedily shall I drink in immortal ease and pleasure! Break away, ye thick clouds! begone, ye envious shades, and let me behold the glories ye conceal: let me see the promised land, and survey the happy regions I am immediately to possess. How long will ye interpose between me and my bright sun — between me and the unclouded face of God? Look up, my soul, see how sweetly those reviving beams break forth! how they dispel the gloom, and gild the shades of death.

※

Elizabeth Rowe (1674–1737), the daughter of a Nonconformist minister, began writing poetry at the age of twelve. Her papers were eventually published under the title *Devout Exercises of the Heart*.

STRENGTHEN ME THIS HOUR

Euphemia of Chalcedon

BLESSED art Thou, O Lord our God, who dwellest in the highest, Thou whom the angels and all the powers of heaven praise and exalt unceasingly. Thy weak and lowly handmaiden calls upon Thee, who regardest the humble: strengthen me this hour with the power of Thy Holy Spirit, and show the wicked enemy . . . that Thou art the God who didst send Thine angel to the three youths and didst drive the flame of fire out of the furnace. Hear my prayer, O Lord; send me Thine aid. Be not mindful of my sins and unworthiness; but, remembering Thy mercy and Thy readiness in helping them that call upon Thee, save me in this hour of my distress.

米

Euphemia of Chalcedon (third century) suffered under the hand of Roman emperor Diocletian and was beheaded for her religious beliefs.

ON THE DEATH OF A YOUNG LADY

Phillis Wheatley

FROM dark abodes to fair etherial light
Th' enraptur'd innocent has wing'd her flight;
On the kind bosom of eternal love
She finds unknown beatitude above.
This know, ye parents, nor her loss deplore,
She feels the iron hand of pain no more;
The dispensations of unerring grace,
Should turn your sorrows into grateful praise;
Let then no tears for her henceforward flow,
No more distress'd in our dark vale below.

※

Phillis Wheatley (1753–1784) began the African-American literary
tradition in 1773 by being the first black woman, and first black person, to publish a book. The name Phillis was taken from the slave
vessel *Phillis* which carried her from the coast of Africa to Boston
Harbor.

Phillis Wheatley

ON TEMPTATIONS

Amanda Smith

WHY does God permit these fierce temptations? It is, I believe, first, to develop the strength and muscle of your own soul and so prepare you for greater service, and second, to bring you into sympathy with others, that are often sorely tempted after they are sanctified, so that you can help them.

BEGINNING OVER AGAIN . . . AND AGAIN

Amelia Barr

T H E desire to begin over again is one of those longings so common and universal that we may say it is a native instinct . . . that we have failed, and failed again and again, need not intimidate us for a new trial. Aspirations, imperfections, and failures are intimations of future achievements. Defeats foretell future successes. The sin to be dreaded is the unlit lamp and ungirt loin. Our light must be burning, however dimly, and we must keep on the right road, however often we stumble on the way. Under no circumstances can it be true that there is not something to be *done*, as well as something to be suffered. Let us sit down before the Lord and count our resources, and see what we are *not* fit for, and give up wishing for it. Let us decide honest what we *can do,* and then do it with all our might.

※

Amelia Barr (1831–1919), the daughter of a Methodist minister, wrote more than seventy-five books. Her short stories were published in such periodicals as *The Christian Union*, *Harper's Bazaar*, and *The Illustrated Christian Weekly*.

A WIDOW'S LAMENTATION

Glückel of Hameln

T H O U knowest well, Almighty God, how I pass my days in trouble and affliction of heart. I was long a woman who stood high in the esteem of her pious husband, who was like the apple of his eye. But with his passing, passed away my treasure and my honor, which all my days and years I now lament and bemoan.

I know that this complaining and mourning is a weakness of mine and a grievous fault. Far better it would be if every day I fell upon my knees and thanked the Lord for the tender mercies He has bestowed on my unworthy self. I sit to this day and date at my own table, eat what I relish, stretch myself at night in my own bed, and have even a shilling to waste, so long as the good God pleases. I have my beloved children, and while things do not always go as well, now with one or the other, as they should, still we are all alive and acknowledge our Creator. How many people there are in this world, finer, better, juster and truer than I, such as I know myself for patterns of piety, who have not bread to put into their mouths! How, then, can I thank and praise my Creator enough for all the goodness He has lavished on us without requital!

If only we poor sinners would acknowledge the everlasting mercy of our God who from the dust of the ground formed us into men, and that we may serve our Creator with all our heart, gave us to know His great and terrible and holy Name!

I AM IN NEED OF A GUIDE

Adelaida Gertsyk

Translated by Sharon Lubkemann Allen

U P H O L D me, Sacred Lord!
Light before me a star —
You see, I am in need of a guide,
Another moment, and I will fall . . .
   I know, I am an unfit, listless slave,
   I was not able to save my home,
   From Your laboring of God's fields
   I did not gather harvest.
And now, in the midst of wasted borderlands
I am a reed shaken by the whirlwind . . .
Lord! You are the host here,
I — your guest . . .
   Release me this night,
   I cannot wait for dawn,
   Release me to my Father's house,
   Open your doors!

※

Adelaida Gertsyk (d. 1925), a deaf Russian Orthodox poet, attempted unsuccessfully to emigrate to Paris after the Russian Revolution. She died in poverty under the Bolshevik regime, in Sudak.

MORE MERCIES THAN AFFLICTIONS

Susanna Wesley

I THANK Thee, O God, because in the whole course of my life there have been more mercies than afflictions and much more pleasure than pain. Though I have suffered pain and bodily infirmities, I have likewise enjoyed great intervals of rest and ease. But all my sufferings, by the admirable management of Thine omnipotent goodness, have concurred to promote my spiritual and eternal good. If, owing to the perverseness of my own will, my frequent lapses into present things and my unfaithfulness to Thy good Spirit, I have failed to reap that advantage of life's adversities which I might have done, I thank Thee because, notwithstanding all my prevarications and all the stupid opposition I have made, Thou hast never totally abandoned me. Glory be to Thee, O Lord!

ONLY WHAT I NEED

Catherine of Genoa

To me every event is God; and whether it be joyful or afflictive, I receive it with equal gratitude, knowing that He will send me only what I need.

To me every object is God. I do not go into distinctions, and say, this is mine, or that is mine. But I say, God is mine; everything belongs to God; and I have an inward conviction, which is better understood than expressed, that in the possession of God I have all that God has.

O my Beloved! is it possible that Thou hast thus called me to Thyself with so great goodness? Is it possible that Thou hast delivered me from my doubt and anguish; and in a moment of time hast imparted a knowledge greater than language can express?

I have faith in Thee, O my God, that Thou wilt not leave me, that Thou wilt not permit me to go astray; but will keep me in all inward thought, as well as in all outward word and action.

☀

Catherine of Genoa (1447–1510) worked for the betterment of the poor. Her resolute devotion to her task eventually inspired her husband — a man of the world — to join her.

MY YEARS OF BANISHMENT

Madame Jeanne Guyon

O Thou, by long experience tried,
Near whom no grief can long abide,
My Lord, how full of sweet content
I pass my years of banishment.

All scenes alike engaging prove
To souls impressed with sacred love;
Where'er they dwell, they dwell in thee,
In heaven, in earth, or on the sea.

To me remains nor place nor time,
My country is in every clime;
I can be calm and free from care
On any shore, since God is there.

While place we seek, or place we shun,
The soul can find repose in none;
But with a God to guide our way,
'Tis equal joy to go or stay.

Could I be cast where thou art not,
That were indeed a dreadful lot;
But regions none remote I call,
Secure of finding God in all.

My country, Lord, art thou alone,
No other can I claim or own —
The point where all my wishes meet,
My law, my love, life's only sweet.

I hold by nothing here below;
Appoint my journey, and I go;
Though pierced by scorn, oppressed by pride,
I feel thee good — feel nought beside.

No frowns of men can hurtful prove
To souls on fire with heavenly love;
Though men and devils both condemn,
No gloomy days arise from them.

Ah, then, to His embrace repair —
My soul, thou art no stranger there;
There love divine shall be thy guard,
And peace and safety thy reward.

ON THE DEATH OF ANNE BRONTË

Charlotte Brontë

T H E R E 's little joy in life for me,
    And little terror in the grave;
I've lived the parting hour to see
    Of one I would have died to save.
Calmly to watch the failing breath,
    Wishing each sigh might be the last;
Longing to see the shade of death
    O'er those beloved features cast.
The cloud, the stillness that must part
    The darling of my life from me;
And then to thank God from my heart,
    To thank Him well and fervently;
Although I knew that we had lost
    The hope and glory of our life;
And now, benighted, tempest-tossed,
    Must bear alone the weary strife.

Charlotte Brontë

ON ADVERSITY

Anne Bradstreet

D o w n y beds make drowsy persons, but hard lodging keeps the eyes open; a prosperous state makes a secure Christian, but adversity makes him consider.

LIGHT TO GUIDE OUR STEPS

George Eliot

As soon as we lay ourselves entirely at His feet, we have enough light given us to guide our own steps; as the foot-soldier, who hears nothing of the councils that determine the course of the great battle he is in, hears plainly enough the word of command which he must himself obey.

※

George Eliot (1819–1880) was the pen name of Mary Ann Evans, the nineteenth-century English writer whose novels include *Silas Marner*, *Mill on the Floss*, and her masterpiece *Middlemarch*.

THE DISGUISE OF GOD

Evelyn Underhill

LORD give me courage and love to open the door and constrain You to enter, whatever the disguise You come in, even before I fully recognize my guest.

Come in! Enter my small life!

Lay Your sacred hands on all the common things and small interests of that life and bless and change them. Transfigure my small resources, make them sacred. And in them give me Your very Self. Amen.

※

THE SPOUSE OF MY SOUL

Rose of Lima

L O R D Jesus Christ, God and Man, my Creator and Saviour, I am extremely sorry and painfully grieved for having offended Thee, because Thou art what Thou art and because I love Thee above all things. My God, who art the Spouse of my soul and all the joy of my heart, I desire, and I desire it with all the power of my being, to love Thee with a very perfect love, with a very efficacious love, with a very sincere ineffable love, the greatest that a creature can have for her God, with an incomprehensible love, with a love resolute and invincible in difficulties; in a word, I desire to love Thee as the saints and angels love Thee in heaven.

※

Rose of Lima (1586–1617), the first Western woman to be canonized, was fond of practicing the art of prayer in her family's flower garden in Lima, Peru.

FORTIFY MY MIND WITH PATIENCE

Susanna Wesley

HELP me, O God, to fortify my mind with patience, submission and renewed repentance, that I may be assured of Divine succours when I most need them. Enable me to live so as to deserve a friend, and if I never have one on earth, be Thou my friend, for in having Thee I shall have all that is dear and valuable in friendship. May I learn by practice to love Thee above all things, that so I may be out of the power of the world and my earthly circumstances give me no uneasiness. I would have my wealth to be Thy favour, with all the blessed consequences attending it; the virtues of Thy Holy Spirit, purifying my mind, exalting my nature to the dignity of a Divine resemblance, teaching me to undervalue whatever a mistaken world calls good, as unnecessary or a hindrance to that spiritual and eternal good which I would prize above all others. . . . Amen.

EPITAPH ON THE DEATH OF MY SON

Katherine Philips

W H A T on Earth deserves our trust?
Youth and Beauty both are dust.
Long we gathering are with pain,
What one moment calls again.
Seven years childless marriage past,
A Son, a son is born at last:
So exactly lim'd and fair,
Full of good Spirits, Meen, and Air,
As a long life promised,
Yet, in less than six weeks dead.
Too promising, too great a mind
In so small room to be confin'd:
Therfore, as fit in Heav'n to dwell,
He quickly broke the Prison shell.
So the subtle Alchimist,
Can't with Hermes Seal resist
The powerful spirit's subtler flight,
But t'will bid him long good night.
And so the Sun if it arise
Half so glorious as his Eyes,
Like this Infant, takes a shrowd,
Buried in a morning Cloud.

⁕

Katherine Philips (1632–1664), a poet and translator of Puritan
descent, died at age thirty-two.

WHY THESE TEARS

Louisa May Alcott

SILENT and sad,
   When all are glad,
And the earth is dressed in flowers;
   When the gay birds sing
   Till the forests ring,
As they rest in woodland bowers.
   Oh, why these tears,
   And these idle fears
For what may come tomorrow?
   The birds find food
   From God so good,
And the flowers know no sorrow.
   If He clothes these
   And the leafy trees,
Will He not cherish thee?
   Why doubt His care;
   It is everywhere,
Though the way we may not see.

※

Louisa May Alcott (1832–1888) is the beloved writer of *Little Women*, a novel of family life published in 1869.

THE GARDEN AS TOUCHSTONE

Emily Herman

WHEN a crisis finds us unready and inadequate to its demands, it is largely because, while we have jostled our brethren along the high-road of religious activity, and kept ourselves busy in the house of organized effort, we have neglected the garden. The glare of the road and the bustle of the house have deceived us. We thought ourselves sterling coin, and when the hand of our Maker rang our metal against the counter of hard fact we were dismayed at the hollow sound. Had we but submitted ourselves to the gentle testing of the garden, we would have escaped this shame. For the garden is a great touchstone. In its clear, quiet light, what passed as gold under the limelight is seen to be tinsel; beside its delicate bloom the pageantry of the public highway appears as so much crude pretentiousness. No soul can remain utterly artificial in the garden of secret fellowship. Its sunshine kills the poison-germ of unreality; its deep quietude lays bare the hidden equivocation, the latent apostasy of our recalcitrant hearts.

WHILE MY DAYS GO ON

Elizabeth Barrett Browning

I PRAISE Thee while my days go on;
I love Thee while my days go on:
Through dark and dearth, through fire and frost,
With emptied arms and treasure lost,
I thank Thee while my days go on.

GIVE ME STRENGTH

Anne Brontë

A DREADFUL darkness closes in
  On my bewildered mind;
O let me suffer and not sin,
  Be tortured yet resigned.
Through all this world of blinding mist
  Still let me look to Thee,
And give me courage to resist
  The Tempter till he flee.
Weary I am, O give me strength
  And leave me not to faint;
Say Thou wilt comfort me at length
  And pity my complaint.
O Thou hast taken my delight
  And hope of life away,
And bid me watch the painful night
  And wait the weary day.
The hope and the delight were Thine:
  I bless Thee for their loan;
I gave Thee while I deemed them mine
  Too little thanks I own.
Shall I with joy Thy blessings share
  And not endure their loss,
Or hope the martyr's Crown to wear
  And cast away the Cross?

Anne Brontë (1820–1849), like sisters Charlotte and Emily, found solace writing verse and story. She published her novel *Agnes Grey* in 1847, under the name Acton Bell.

FAITH AND ABSOLUTE SOLUTIONS

Flannery O'Connor

WHERE you have absolute solutions, however, you have no need of faith.

※

Flannery O'Connor (1925–1969) was the Southern novelist who wrote *Wise Blood* and *Everything That Rises Must Converge*. Along with Dostoevsky's, her work is considered a supreme example of modern fiction written from a theological perspective.

LOVE LARGELY AND HATE NOTHING

Ella Wheeler Wilcox

USE all your hidden forces. Do not miss
The purpose of this life, and do not wait
For circumstance to mold or change your fate.
In your own self lies destiny. Let this
Vast truth cast out all fear, all prejudice,
All hesitation. Know that you are great,
Great with divinity. So dominate
Environment, and enter into bliss.
Love largely and hate nothing. Hold no aim
That does not chord with universal good.
Hear what the voices of the silence say,
All joys are yours if you put forth your claim,
Once let the spiritual laws be understood.
Material things must answer and obey.

Ella Wheeler Wilcox (1850–1919), a poet and journalist, claimed
that her mother's frequent recitation of Shakespeare helped shape
her literary career.

A BALLAD

Anne Askew

L y k e as the armed knyght
Appoynted to the fielde
With thys world wyll I fyght
And fayth shall be my shielde.

Faythe is that weapon stronge
Whych wyll not fayle at nede
My foes therfor amonge
Therwith wyll I procede.

As it is had in strengthe
And force of Christes waye
It wyll prevayle at lengthe
Though all the devyls saye naye.

Faythe in the fathers olde
Obtayned ryghtwysnesse
Whych make me verye bolde
To feare no worldes dystresse.

I now rejoyce in hart
And hope byd me do so
For Christ wyll take my part
And ease me of my wo.

Thu sayst lorde, who so knocke
To them wylt thu attende
Undo therfor the locke
And thy stronge power sende.

More enmyes now I have
Than heeres upon my heed
Lete them not me deprave
But fyght thu in my steed.

On the my care I cast
For all their cruell spyght

I sett not by their hast
For thu art my delyght.

    I am not she that lyst
My anker to lete fall
For everye dryslynge myst
My shyppe substancyall.

    Nor oft use I to wryght
In prose nor yet in ryme
Yet wyll I shewe ne syght
That I sawe in my tyme.

    I sawe a ryall trone
Where Justyce shuld have sytt
But in her stede was one
Of modye cruell wytt.

    Absorpt was rygtwysnesse
As of the ragynge floude
Sathan in his excesse
Sucte up the gyltelesse bloude.

    Then thought I, Jesus lorde
Whan thu shalt judge us all
Harde is it to recorde
On these men what wyll fall.

    Yet lorde I the desyre
For that they do to me
Lete them not taste the hyre
Of their inyquyte.

Anne Askew (1521–1546) was an English martyr who was tortured and burned at the stake for her views on the sacraments. Her experience and martyrdom were written about by John Foxe in his 1563 *Book of Martyrs*.

QUENCH THIS VOICELESS THIRST

Anna Akhmatova

Translated by Sharon Lubkemann Allen

Thus I prayed: "Quench
This voiceless thirst of poetry!"
But for the earthly there is no escaping earth
And there was no deliverance.

As smoke from a sacrifice, that cannot
Ascend to the throne of Might and Glory,
But only drift at its foot,
Imploringly kissing the grass —

Thus, I, Lord, fall prostrate:
Will the heavenly fire touch
My closed eyelashes
And my wondrous muteness?

THIS WORLD IS NOT CONCLUSION

Emily Dickinson

T H I S world is not conclusion;
　　A sequel stands beyond,
Invisible, as music,
　　But positive, as sound.
It beckons and it baffles;
　　Philosophies don't know,
And through a riddle, at the last,
　　Sagacity must go.
To guess it puzzles scholars;
　　To gain it, men have shown
Contempt of generations,
　　And crucifixion known.

PART FIVE

A Legacy of Wisdom

HOLY MYSTERIES

Elizabeth Barrett Browning

GOD keeps His holy mysteries
   Just on the outside of man's dream;
In diapason slow, we think
To hear their pinions rise and sink,
While they float pure beneath His eyes,
   Like swans adown a stream.
Abstractions, are they, from the forms
   Of His great beauty? — exaltations
From His great glory? — strong previsions
Of what we shall be? — intuitions
Of what we are — in calms and storms
   Beyond our peace and passions?
Things nameless! Which, in passing so,
   Do stroke us with a subtle grace;
We say, "Who passes?" — they are dumb;
We cannot see them go or come,
Their touches fall soft, cold, as snow
   Upon a blind man's face.
Yet, touching so they draw above
   Our common thoughts to Heaven's unknown;
Our daily joy and pain advance
To a divine significance,
Our human love — O mortal love,
   That light is not its own!

PRAYER HAS GREAT POWER

Mechthilde of Magdeburg

THAT prayer has great power
Which a person makes with all his might
It makes a sour heart sweet,
    A sad heart merry,
    A poor heart rich,
    A foolish heart wise,
    A timid heart brave,
    A sick heart well,
    A blind heart full of sight,
    A cold heart ardent.
It draws down the great God into the little heart,
It drives the hungry soul up into the fullness of God.
It brings together two lovers,
    God and the soul,
In a wondrous place where they speak much of love.

THOUGHTS ON PROVIDENCE

Phillis Wheatley

ARISE, my soul, on wings enraptur'd rise
To praise the monarch of the earth and skies,
Whose goodness and beneficence appear
As round its centre moves the rolling year,
Or when the morning glows with rosy charms,
Or the sun slumbers in the ocean's arms:
Of light divine be a rich portion lent
To guide my soul, and favour my intent.
Celestial muse, my arduous flight sustain,
And raise my mind to a seraphic strain!

ON BEING JEWISH

Golda Meir

To me, being Jewish means and has always meant being proud to be part of a people that has maintained its distinct identity for more than two thousand years, with all the pain and torment that have been inflicted upon it. Those who have been unable to endure and who have tried to opt out of their Jewishness have done so, I believe, at the expense of their own basic identity. They have pitifully impoverished themselves.

I don't know what forms the practice of Judaism will assume in the future or how Jews, in Israel and elsewhere, will express their Jewishness one thousand years hence. But I do know that Israel is not just some small beleaguered country in which three million people are trying hard to survive; Israel is a Jewish state that has come into existence as the result of the longing, the faith and determination of an ancient people. We in Israel are only one part of the Jewish nation, and not even its largest part; but because Israel exists Jewish history has been changed forever, and it is my deepest conviction that there are few Israelis today who do not understand and fully accept the responsibility that history has placed on their shoulders as Jews.

※

Golda Meir (1898–1978), née Goldie Mabovitch, was the Jewish émigré to Palestine from the Ukraine who helped found the modern State of Israel and became its fourth prime minister.

A GREAT AND SILENT FORCE

Ray Frank

T H E weaker sex physically, it is the stronger spiritually, it having been said that religion were impossible without woman. And yet the freedom of the human soul has been apparently effected by man. I say apparently effected, for experience has demonstrated, and history records, that one element possessed by woman has made her the great moral, the great motif force of the world, though she be, as all great forces are, a silent force.

IF WE CANNOT HEAR THE CAROL

Willa Cather

U P in the Negro church one Christmas the congregation were singing the "Peace on Earth." When the plaintive music stopped an old gray-haired Negro in a frock coat and wearing two pairs of glasses arose and began reading the old, old story of the men who were watching their flocks by night and of the babe who was born in the city of David. He became very much excited as he read, and his voice trembled and he unconsciously put the words to measure and chanted them slowly. When he finished he looked up at the ceiling with eager misty eyes as though he could see the light of the heavenly messenger shining in upon him. It is a beautiful story, this, of holiest and purest childhood on earth, beautiful even to those who cannot understand it, as dreams are sweet to men without hope. After all, if we cannot hear the carol and see the heavenly messenger, it is because our ears are deaf and our eyes are blind, not that we turn willfully away from love or beauty. No one is antagonistic by preference. Almost any one of us who doubt would give the little we know or hope to know to go down upon our knees among the lowly and experience a great faith or a great conviction.

Willa Cather (1873–1947), the American novelist who wrote *My Antonia* and *Death Comes for the Archbishop*, experienced a personal and spiritual renaissance after joining the Episcopal Church. Cather's fiction demonstrates her belief that the pursuit of God is humanity's highest possibility.

ON PRAYER

Madame Jeanne Guyon

H E who has a pure heart will never cease to pray; and he who will be constant in prayer, shall know what it is to have a pure heart.

THE PROPHETIC VISION

Josephine Lazarus

. . . W E stand upon the threshold of we know not what, — unable to go backward, not daring to go forward. The future beckons us on with promise of wider, freer life, unchecked growth and scope, broad, unhampered human and spiritual fellowship. The past holds us with invincible weight. "Deny me, and you deny yourself," it says, "your very life, all that makes you what you are." The blood of martyrs seems to cry to us: "Would you be faithless, then to us, and have we died in vain?"

And whence come these questionings, this doubt and division of soul? Surely from lack of faith and vision, rather than from true loyalty and conviction. Not in vain will be that martyrdom when it has taught us to be faithful as those martyrs were and when we have, as they had, a faith of our own to be true to; when we are ready to trust and follow it wherever it may lead, to deny self and offer up life for its sake. But we have lost the faith, not merely in the narrow historic sense, not alone in allegiance to the past, in outward conformity to external rites and inherited usage, but as an inward, quickening power, a source of our spiritual life and action, a vision of something that makes life holy, beautiful, and blessed, whatever martyrdom we may be called upon to endure, whatever sacrifice we may be called upon to make.

And when we read it aright, the history of our people means, above all else this faith, a perfect trust and confidence in the leading and purpose of the Most High, whatever that leading and purpose may be, and whether or not we understand it. . . .

Whether or not we have the prophetic vision, whether or not we see and understand the promise beyond, we can be faithful still, now that we find ourselves on the verge of a larger deliverance than ever before. They are the faithless who would lag behind.

※

Josephine Lazarus (1846–1910), an American writer, urged unity among women of the Jewish and Christian faiths based on their historical and theological connectedness. She expressed her vision in *The Spirit of Judaism*, a collection of essays published in 1895.

MY FEAR OF WHITE PEOPLE

Amanda Smith

S O M E H O W I always had a fear of white people — that is, I was not afraid of them in the sense of doing me harm, or anything of that kind — but a kind of fear because they were white, and were there, and I was black, and was here! But that morning on Green street, as I stood on my feet trembling, I heard these words distinctly. They seemed to come from the northeast corner of the church, slowly, but clearly: "There is neither Jew nor Greek, there is neither bond nor free, there is neither male nor female, for ye are all one in Christ Jesus." (Galatians 3:28.) I never understood that text before. But now the Holy Ghost had made it clear to me. And as I looked at white people that I had always seemed to be afraid of, now they looked so small. The great mountain had become a molehill. "Therefore, if the Son shall make you free, then are you free, indeed." All praise to my victorious Christ!

⁂

MUCH TO HOPE FOR

Anne Plato

H o w many of us are able to say that we are persuaded that neither life nor death, nor things present, nor things to come, nor height, nor depth, nor any other creature, shall be able to separate us from the love of God. . . . Religion confers on the mind principles of noble independence. "The upright man is satisfied from himself"; he despises not the advantages of fortune, but he centers not his happiness in them. With a moderate share of them he can be contented; and contentment is felicity. Happy in his own integrity, conscious of the esteem of good men, reposing firm trust in providence, and the promises of God, he is exempted from servile dependence on other things. He can wrap himself up in a good conscience, and look forward, without terror, to the change of the world. Let all things fluctuate around him as they please, that by the Divine ordination, they shall be made to work together in the issue, for his good; and therefore, having much to hope from God, and little to fear from the world, he can be easy in every state. One who possesses within himself such an establishment of mind, is truly free.

※

Anne Plato (c. 1820–?) was the second black woman to publish a book. A schoolteacher, she published her *Essays, Including Biographies and Miscellaneous Pieces in Prose and Poetry* in 1841.

GOD NEVER CHANGES

Teresa of Avila

Let nothing disturb thee,
Nothing affright thee;
All things are passing;
God never changes;
Patient endurance
Attaineth to all things;
Who God possesseth
In nothing is wanting;
Alone God sufficeth.

RUTH

Elizaveta Kuzmina-Karavaeva

Translated by Sharon Lubkemann Allen

I GATHERED the ears in my skirt,
Walked barefoot through alien stubble;
As above the huts of the village
Flew a braided chain of cranes.

And I slipped through the dark blue fog
Far from the plains of Boaz;
And I traveled through unfamiliar countries
Wrapped in my shawl against the frost.

And the crane, flying South,
Will tell nobody, nobody,
How from the harvest abandoned in the field
Ruth weaves golden sheaves.

As soon as the brief day breaks,
And the harvester leaves for work,
On the plains of a foreign countryside
Ruth begins her golden hunt.

She lowers her scarf on her brow,
So as not to betray her southern braids,
Gathers her scattered sheaves,
Wanders every hill and slope.

And having crossed the threshold in winter,
Old women often, through the morning cold,
Notice in the snow, at their feet,
A sheaf of unthreshed corn . . .

※

Elizaveta Kuzmina-Karavaeva (d. 1945) was the first Russian
Orthodox woman to study theology at St. Petersburg Theological
Academy. After the revolution, she emigrated to Paris and took the
vows of Orthodoxy. She participated in the French Resistance until
she was deported to the Ravensbruck concentration camp, where
she died in 1945.

Ruth and Naomi

WISE SAYINGS

Anne Bradstreet

SWEET words are like honey: a little may refresh, but too much gluts the stomach.

•

THE finest bread hath the least bran, the purest honey the least wax, and the sincerest Christian the least self-love.

•

AUTHORITY without wisdom is like a heavy axe without an edge: fitter to bruise than polish.

SEEK SOLITUDE AND PRAY

Joan of Arc

WERE it not for God's grace I could do nothing. Had I not the assurance that God directs my work, I would rather tend sheep than expose myself to such great perils.

If I am not in God's grace, may God bring me there; if I am in it, may He keep me there. I should be of all creatures the most miserable if I knew myself not to be in God's grace.

When I am in any way opposed, because men will hardly believe that what I declare has come from God, I seek solitude and pray to God, lamenting to Him that they to whom I speak will not readily believe me. When my prayer to God is ended, I hear a Voice that says to me: "Daughter of God, go, go, go; I will be thy helper, go!" and when I hear this voice, I have great joy; indeed, I would I could hear it always.

※

Joan of Arc (1412–1431), patroness of France, is remembered for her courage and patriotism. She was burned at the stake for her religious beliefs.

ANOTHER YEAR IS DAWNING

Francis Ridley Havergal

A N O T H E R year is dawning:
　　Dear Master, let it be,
In working or in waiting,
　　Another year with thee.

Another year of leaning
　　Upon thy loving breast,
Of ever-deepening trustfulness,
　　Of quiet, happy rest.

Another year of mercies,
　　Of faithfulness and grace;
Another year of gladness
　　In the shining of thy face.

Another year of progress;
　　Another year of praise;
Another year of proving
　　Thy presence "all the days."

Another year of service,
　　Of witness for thy love;
Another year of training
　　For holier work above.

Another year is dawning:
Dear Master, let it be,
On earth, or else in heaven,
Another year for thee.

Francis Ridley Havergal (1836—1879), an English hymnwriter, mastered Hebrew and Greek in order to read the Old and New Testaments of the Bible in the original.

CULTIVATING FAITH

Flannery O'Connor

I F you want your faith, you have to work for it. It is a gift, but for very few is it a gift given without any demand for equal time devoted to its cultivation.

HELPS AND HINDRANCES

Madame Jeanne Guyon

W H A T is a help to perfection at one time, is a hindrance at another; what formerly helped you in your way to God, will now prevent your reaching Him; the more wants we have, the further we are from God, and the nearer we approach him, the better can we dispense with everything that is not Himself. When we have come there, we use everything indifferently, and have no more need but of Him.

THE DAYS OF MIRACLES ARE NOT PAST

Amanda Smith

T H E days of miracles are not past. God has healed without the use of means of any kind, as well as with; and why He does not now heal every case as He used to do, I do not think I have any right to say is because of a lack of faith on the part of some poor, weak child of God; and so consign them to perdition. Then there are some things God would have us do for ourselves. Not long ago I was at the home of a good minister, a man that knew the Lord, and for years had walked in the light and blessedness of full salvation. He had begun to get deaf in his right ear; it came on gradually; sometimes worse than at other times. So he prayed earnestly, and believed God, and held on about a year. Finally he seemed to grow worse. His wife, a good, saved, orthodox, level-headed woman, had often said to him he ought to see a doctor about it. But he had a pretty strong will of his own, and did not yield easily to her persuasions. But she was gentle and patient. One morning as he was sitting in the room talking with me, she came in and said, "Now, my dear, you must really go and see the doctor this morning about your deafness; let him examine it; you are getting worse all the time, and it will never do to have you going around deaf."

The good man looked at his wife, then he turned to me and said, smilingly, "Sister Smith, my wife is generally pretty clear when she decides upon a thing."

"Yes, Sister Smith," she said, "it would do no harm to go and see about it, anyhow."

"Sister M.," I said, "You are quite right; just what I say."

So off he went. He was gone about two hours. When he returned, I said, "Well, Brother M., what did the doctor say?"

"Oh! Praise the Lord," he said, "I am all right; clear as a bell." So he told the story, and laughed heartily. I said, "What did the doctor do?"

"Oh," he said, "he told me to sit down and he would examine my ear; he said there was nothing serious the matter; the wax was very dry. So he took his instruments and took out about a thimbleful of wax, and put a little sweet oil or something in it, and it is all right."

"Yes," I said, "praise the Lord. Some people would have teased the Lord to have Him clean out their ears, when they might do it themselves, or get someone to do it to whom God had given the sense and ability."

DO NOT STAY IN THE GARDEN

Emily Herman

B u t if many are tempted to ignore the garden, many tend to dwell in it so exclusively as to turn its refreshing quietude into an enervating narcotic. The garden has an irresistible attraction for peace-loving souls. It is so delightful to shut the gate and forget the struggles and contentions, the burning questions and searching issues, which meet the soul on life's highway. It is easy to be sweet and gentle in the garden, easy to cast controversy to the winds and give oneself up to spiritual consolations and raptures. It is possible for a sincerely devout soul to shine in the garden, but to prove itself ineffective on the high-road; to excel in the devotional life, but fail to translate its devotion into terms of social righteousness.

RELIGION AS THE DAUGHTER OF HEAVEN

Anne Plato

RELIGION is the daughter of Heaven — parent of our virtues, and source of all true felicity. She alone giveth peace and contentment; divests the heart of anxious cares, bursts on the mind a flood of joy, and sheds unmingled and preternatural sunshine in the pious breast. By her the spirits of darkness are banished from the earth, and angelic ministers of grace thicken, unseen, the regions of mortality. She promotes love and good will among men — lifts up the head that hangs down — heals the wounded spirit — dissipates the gloom of sorrow — sweetens the cup of affliction — blunts the sting of death, and whatever seen, felt and enjoyed, breathes around her an everlasting spring.

Religion raises men above themselves: irreligion sinks them beneath the brutes. The one makes them angels; the other makes them evil spirits. *This* binds them down to a poor pitiable speck of perishable earth; *that* opens up a vista to the skies, and lets loose all the principles of an immortal mind, among the glorious objects of an eternal world.

GOD'S GIFTS, GOD'S GRACES

Madame Jeanne Guyon

GOD gives us gifts, graces, and natural talents, not for our own use, but that we may render them to Him. He takes pleasure in giving and in taking them away, or in so disposing of us, that we cannot enjoy them; but their grand use is to be offered in a continual sacrifice to Him; and by this He is most glorified.

CLOSER TO FINAL TRUTH

Adelaida Gertsyk

Translated by Sharon Lubkemann Allen

T H E Y give us cold, wise books,
And in each He is spoken of differently.
They interpret Him with prophetic words,
And each interprets Him in its own way.
And each word about Him — is an insult to me,
And each book — a fresh wound,
The more things prophesied about Him,
The less I know the plain truth.
When His inflicting speech falls silent,
My heart is eaten away by life's . . .
As a bird whose wings have been severed,
Or a house abandoned by its host.
And only the candles facing the icons,
Shimmering, know the most essential,
And their flickering light,
Their humble, unanswerable burning
Leads closer to final truth.

※

I HAVE ONLY TODAY

Thérèse of Lisieux

M Y life is an instant,
An hour which passes by;
My life is a moment
Which I have no power to stay.
You know, O my God,
That to love you here on earth —
I have only today.

A GUIDE TO THE READINGS

INDEX OF AUTHORS

ACKNOWLEDGMENTS

My life has been influenced by many individuals, living and dead. For their role in helping me give birth to this book I acknowledge the following:

Jennifer, Landon, Bailey, and Madison—my four loves. I am rich because of you.

David Smith, my agent, who did his work quickly.

David Dakkers Allen, my foremost critic and ultimately my friend.

Pamela McClure, my publicist, who is certainly one of the top religion professionals working today.

Billy Graham, Fr. Richard John Neuhaus, Max Lucado, Charles Colson, and the other talented authors whose books I've been fortunate to design. Each project was pure joy.

Susan Gehrlein and Dawn Letson of Texas Woman's University Library welcomed me into their outstanding Woman's collection and guided me through the Edith Dean archives.

My former colleagues at Word Publishing: Theta Irene Hall, Sabra, Kelli, Kathryn, and Debbie; David Moberg, Jack Countryman, Terri Gibbs, and Laura Llevarino.

Alyse Lounsberry at Creation House, who offered kind words of encouragement.

My engaging editor, Lisa Kaufman, whose fondness for this project never wavered but in fact grew. Best wishes at PublicAffairs.

The little girls of El Campo who always returned my focus to the here-and-now.

Andrew "Junior Boy" Jones and Shirley Jones, Ronnie and Trish Bramhall, Tommy Hill, and Tommy Tucker, who continue to expand my soul with their Texas blues.

Daddy "Jack" Chaplin whose Dallas lobster and chowder house serves some of the Southwest's best seafood.

Jimmy DePetris, my horseshoe buddy, whose "win-win" credo has rubbed off on me.

Siri Hutcheson, who invited me more than once to her haven of rest in Wimberly, Texas, so I could finish this book.

Patricia "Pat-Pat" Hutcheson, who loves my children unwaveringly.

My new friends and colleagues at Taylor Publishing, where hardback books are still Smythe sewn.

Sharon Lubkemann Allen, artist and occasional translator, is without question the most brilliant woman I know. Your art and your words have transformed this book. Gracias.

Grateful acknowledgment is made to the following for permission to quote copyrighted material:

Moyer Bell, for permission to quote from *The Simone Weil Reader,* edited by George A. Panichas.

Excerpts from *The Habit of Being: The Letters of Flannery O'Connor,* edited by Sally Fitzgerald. Copyright © 1979 by Regina O'Connor. Reprinted by permission of Farrar, Straus & Giroux, Inc.

Quotation from *A Gift for God* by Mother Teresa. Copyright © 1975 by Mother Teresa Missionaries of Charity. Reprinted by permission of HarperCollins Publishers, Inc.

Excerpts from *My Life* reprinted by permission of the Putnam Publishing Group. Copyright © 1975 by Golda Meir.

Excerpts from *A Simple Path* by Mother Teresa © 1975 by Mother Teresa Missionaries of Charity.

A Woman's Book of Faith is set in Eric Gill's Perpetua family of typefaces.

Pencil drawings by Sharon Allen were scanned on a Linotype-Hell flatbed scanner using Linocolor software. Additional image editing was done using Adobe Photoshop version 4.0.

Printed and bound by
Rose Printing Company.

Book design by M. Shawn McGarry.